CW01390401

MEDITERRANEO EDITIONS

Arkadi
The Historic Monastery

Text by
STELLA KALOGERAKI
Archaeologist

Layout
VANGELIS PAPIOMYTOGLOU

Photographs
VANGELIS PAPIOMYTOGLOU, GIORGOS MARKOULAKIS

Translation
JOHN O'SHEA

Translation coordinated by: COM
N. PRATSINIS & K. ZISSIMOU LTD.
www.pra-zis.gr

Copyright 2002, 2007
MEDITERRANEO EDITIONS
Tel. +3028310 21590, Fax: +3028310 21591

www.mediterraneo.gr

ISBN: 960-8227-21-6

Arkadi

The Historic Monastery

C O N T E N T S

THE LOCATION
OF THE
MONASTERY

Agios Dimitrios Church

At an altitude of almost 500 meters and a distance of some 23 kilometers from the city of Rethymnon lies the Monastery of Arkadi set among the northwestern foothills of Mount Ida or Psiloritis. Several routes can be followed to reach the Monastery, each of which is of historical interest allowing one to see different aspects of the Cretan natural landscape.

The route which passes through *Rethymnon, Adele, Pigi, Loutra, Amnatos and Arkadi* allows the traveller to cross the endless olive grove in the area of Adele, Crete's largest and one of the most extensive in the entire Mediterranean; to take a detour, if wished, immediately after the village of Pigi to the village of Agios Dimitrios with its domed cruciform Byzantine church with the same name, and continuing along the primary route to stop in the historical village of Amnatos to marvel at the Venetian gateway with the inscription "It is wise to fear the Lord". On the last leg of the journey towards the Monastery which passes through the Arkadiotiko Gorge the traveller

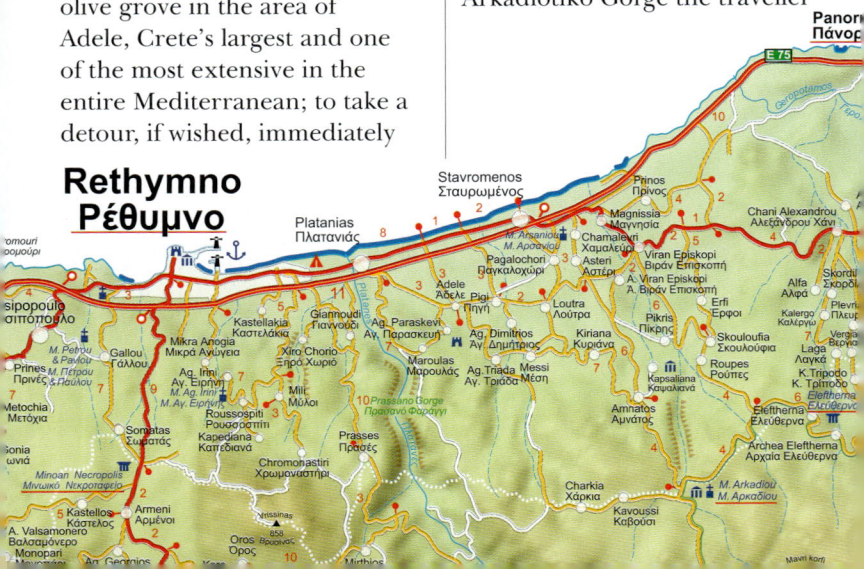

A Venetian door at Amnato

A Venetian gateway at Pikri

will be greeted with impressive images of the wild Cretan nature with all manner of bushes, trees and aromatic plants.

On the second route which passes from *Rethymnon, Stavromenos, Magnisia, Viran Episkopi, Roupes* and ends at *Arkadi*, it is worth taking a slight

detour to the village of Ano Viran Episkopi where on can visit the Byzantine Basilica of Agios Dimitrios and to the village of Pikri with its plethora of Venetian architectural elements while there is ample recompense for having taken this route when, on the approach to Arkadi, one is suddenly confronted with

The tanneries (Tabakaria)

the plateau where the historical Monastery is built covered as it is with cypress trees, hollies, pines and olive trees.

Regardless of the route the visitor chooses to follow to arrive at the historical Monastery, having completed the tour of the Monastery's grounds, it is possible to return to Rethymnon by following an exceptional rambling path which passes through the Arkadiotiko Gorge. The gorge, which begins from the old bridge at the location known as Tambakaria, ends in the area of Stavromenos, east

In Arkadiotiko Gorge in addition to the wonderful fauna one can also admire unique fossils.

The plateau with the monastery as seen from Korres Hill topped by Holy Cross Church (above).

of the city of Rethymnon. At the beginning of the route one can see constructions directly related to the Monastery which have been wholly or partially preserved. These include a stone bridge, a water fountain and a tannery. In all likelihood the Monastery's water supply came from this fountain. The ruins of a domed building are part of the tannery where the monks treated animal pelts in order to produce leather for their shoes. If one wants to continue the route by foot via the gorge, having toured the area around the mouth of the gorge, it is better to return to the plateau where the Monastery is situated and to head northeast following the edge of Korres Hill with the Church of the Holy Cross (Timios Stavros) on it and to re-enter the gorge from there. To the right amid the towering cypress trees one will then see the ruins of a Monastery. This location is known as Astyrakia.

Of note too are the water mills along the length of the course of the Arkadioti River. All those interested in flora will find themselves in a true paradise since a tremendous variety of plants and wild flowers are endemic to the Arkadiotiko Gorge.

Apart from the interesting routes leading to the Monastery and the Arkadiotiko Gorge itself, we ought also to refer to the wider area around Arkadi which ism beyond doubt, a singularly important region. In addition to the exceptionally beautiful natural landscape that this region is endowed with, its proximity to what was in antiquity the sacred Mount Ida, the mountain chosen in order to bring up the father of the gods, Zeus, has

played an important role in its development. An indisputable example of this proximity and correlation is the ancient city of Eleftherna which neighbours the Monastery. This city not only flourished during the time of Homer and the Classical and Roman periods but also retained a strong presence even during the Paleo-Christian and Byzantine periods. The importance of the wider area is undoubtedly to be evidenced in the villages which developed, primarily in the region southeast of Arkadi. A brief excursion into the area is enough for one to explore the rich remains of the Byzantine age, Venetian rule and the modern period. Byzantine chapels, Venetian door-frames and buildings constructed in line with the principles of traditional Cretan architecture frequently co-exist in perfect harmony, indicating not only that this landscape was never abandoned but also that each generation erected building in perfect respect for those of its predecessors.

On the road to Arkadi just before the plateau lies the church of Panagia Mercouri on the right and the remains of a dependency of Arkadi monastery with the same name which was founded by Abbot Neophytos Drosas. It was used by nuns.

◀ *The forest of pine trees.*

Inside the gorge is an area known as Astyrakia which took its name from the wealth of flowers (Styrax) which thrive in the area. In this heavenly garden apart from the church dedicated to the Virgin are the ruins of a small village where nuns lived. This undoubtedly was controlled by Arkadi Monastery.

THE
REVOLUTION
OF 1866-1869 &
THE ARKADI
DRAMA

According to tradition, the Monastery of Arkadi was founded by Byzantine Emperor Heraclius and was rebuilt by Emperor Arcadius in the 5th century AD from whom the Monastery took its name. However, academic opinion supports the view that the Monastery was both founded and took its name, giving the wider area its name too, from some monk by the name of Arcadius, since the tactic of a monk founding a Monastery and attributing his name to it was normal and was done with other monasteries on Crete such as the Arsani and Vrontisi monasteries, among others.

The evidence available about the dating of the Monastery comes from inscriptions and documentary sources. With some certainty we can say that the two-aisled church which dominates the centre of the Monastery was erected in 1587. We can see this much from an inscription uncovered at the base of the bell tower at a time when the abbot was Climis Hortatsis. The Monastery was then dedicated to the Transfiguration of Christ the Saviour and to the Byzantine saints Constantine and Helen, to whom the Monastery's first church had been dedicated as we shall see below. Construction of the second church during a period of intense intellectual and artistic creativity required the design and building of a monument which would stand apart for its magnificence.

The inscription at the base of the bell tower reads CLIMIS HORTAZIS 1587.

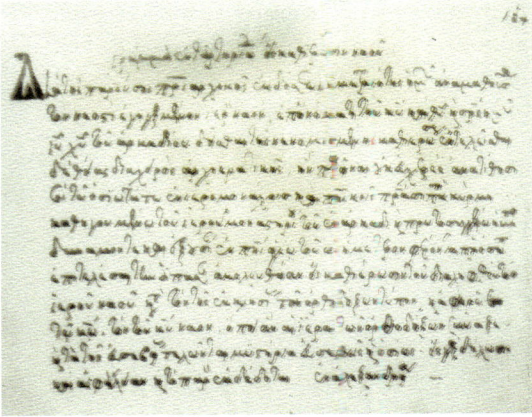

The letter from the Patriarch of Alexandria, Meletius Pigas to the Abbot of the Monastery granting him the authority to undertake the official opening of the church. A copy of the original letter which has not survived is to be found in the library of the Patriarchate of Alexandria.

Moreover, the abbot, Climis Hortatsis, whose name is to be found in abbreviated form in the bell tower inscription (ΚΛΜ ΧΤΖ), undoubtedly belonged to the well-known Rethymnon family, the Hortatsides, whose name has been closely linked with the Cretan Renaissance. Tradition has it that rebuilding of the church took 25 years and thus we must assume that work began around 1562.

As mentioned above, the church we see today is not the original structure but a renovation of the previous one. This was confirmed by the researcher K. Kalokyris who in 1951 discovered and published a 14th century inscription according to which the Monastery was called Arkadi and its church was dedicated to Saint Constantine. The precise wording of the inscription is as follows:

ΑΡΚΑ]ΔΙ (ΟΝ) ΚΕΚΛΗΜΑΙ
ΝΑΟΝ ΗΔ' ΕΧΩ
ΚΩΝΣΤΑΝΤΙΝΟ]Υ ΑΝΑΚΤΟΣ
ΙΣΑΠΟΣΤΟΛΟΥ

THE CHURCH IS CALLED ARKADI AND IT IS DEDICATED TO ST. CONSTANTINE

Another interesting piece of information is that which tells us that Arkadi was transformed into a coenobitic Monastery in 1572. At that time the abbot continued to be Climis Hortatsis. Evidence for this comes from a notarial deed published by Konstantinos D. Mertzios in 1961.

Abbot Climis Hortatsis, whose name is connected with what are perhaps two of the most important works at the Monastery, its conversion into a coenobitic Monastery in 1572 and the construction of the new church of the Saviour in 1587, must have died immediately after completion of these works thus explaining why he did not manage to officially open the new church. Research by Prof. M. I. Manousakas has brought to light an important letter from the Patriarch of

Alexandria, Meletius Pigas, according to which Hortatsis' successor, Abbot Mitrophanes Tsyrigos, was assigned the task of performing the church opening ceremony. The letter is undated but according to the researcher it should not be placed before 1590, the year in which Pigas was invested as Patriarch or after 1596 when Abbot Mitrophanes Tsyrigos was succeeded by Abbot Nikiphorus. Consequently, during this period the final details on the church were completed and it began to be used.

Under its first three abbots and in the period which followed up until the 17th century Arkadi flourished in economic and spiritual terms, as can be ascertained from the fact that it was an important centre for copying manuscripts. Some of these manuscripts are located in libraries abroad but most, which were located in the Monastery's library, were destroyed during its own holocaust. Destruction of the Monastery and its library with the manuscripts followed a more general cultural downturn under Ottoman rule although the abbots never ceased their efforts to revive the Monastery, so that it once again acquired its own glory.

Beyond any doubt it was the leading role that the Monastery played during the **1866-1869 revolution** that led to Arkadi becoming established as the historic symbol of self-sacrifice and liberty.

Let us take events as they unfolded.

According to evidence from the poet of the Cretan War, Marinos Tzanes Bouniales, the Turks, following the fall of Rethymnon in 1669 poured into the countryside where among other things they looted Arkadi. Following this the monks and the Monastery's Abbot Symeon Halkiopoulos, who had sought refuge in Vrontisi Monastery, having declared their allegiance to Hussein Pasha, requested that he allow them to return to their Monastery. In fact the Turks not only allowed them to return to the Monastery but also conceded them the right to sound their bell, a fact which give rise to the new name for the Monastery used by the Turks **'Tsandli Monastir'** (Monastery where the bell rings). The normal sounding of the bell for a period of four years and the reconstruction of new cells and walls around the courtyard

The old seal of the Monastery (1765)

during that period was later to be a source of displeasure to Mustafa Pasha who ordered an on-site investigation to ascertain whether what were, in his view, illegalities were in fact going on. It was proven that the right to sound the bell had been conceded by Hussein Pasha. As far as reconstruction of the cells and courtyard was concerned, this was due to a misinterpretation of the firman that had been issued for the restoration of ruined monasteries based on their original plans without additions and changes. It was this breach of permission at Arkadi Monastery that displeased the Pasha and led to a search for the monks responsible. A series of Turkish documents provide information about the taxation system, the finances of the Monastery and its inner life. Thus we learn that the Abbot Neophytos Drósas, Drosás or Drosakis was succeeded by his nephew Methodius in the year 1717. Methodius was later accused of poor conduct and of illegal possession of the property of a deceased monk, accusations which the ecclesiastical court dismissed.

According to evidence, in 1822 a group of Turks from Rethymnon led by the unscrupulous Yetimali broke into Arkadi, seized and looted it but not for long since within a short time residents from the area of Amari had devised a plan and managed to annihilate Yetilmali and his followers, to the great chagrin of the Turks.

From 1858 onwards the situation worsened and relations between the Christians and the Turks heightened continuously with the latter ignoring their

Arkadi depicted in a copper engraving of that time

HADJI MICHALIS GIANNARIS

Hadji Michalis Giannaris, chief of the Kydon province and head of the Committee for Improving the State and Condition of Christians, reached Arkadi and organized a meeting below its historic oak tree. There he stressed the need for collaboration between the regions of Crete in order to ensure a return of their privileges by the Sultan. For this reason he proposed the election of a revolutionary committee which would cooperate with the island's General Assembly. Abbot Gabriel Marinakis was elected as chairman of this revolutionary committee based at Arkadi Monastery.

promises and taking ever more severe measures against the Orthodox Christians.

In 1866 the Christians of Crete decided to react. Their gathering at Omalo and the preparation of a report to the Sultan in which, inter alia, they requested recognition of the right of religious tolerance, a right which in the past had been granted by the Turks, led to even greater tension in their relations. At the next general meeting held in the village of Askyfo in Skafia it was decided that Turkish authority in Crete would no longer be recognized and unification of Crete with Greece would be sought. As a result of these decision it was now clear that armed conflict would be unavoidable. The Turks did in fact send an army to Crete, secured military reinforcements from Egypt and began attacks against various strategic locations in the countryside. On the other hand, the Cretans, supported by the rest of Greece, threw themselves with a passion into one revolutionary activity after the other. Their aim was to cast off the Turkish yoke while at the same time ensuring national and religious independence. The spread of the revolution into the Rethymnon area was ensured by the General Assembly held at Arkadi chaired by Hadji Michalis Giannaris. In one of his speeches he sought to ignite the patriotism and indignation of the Cretans

20

ABBOT GABRIEL

Abbot Gabriel Marinakis was born in Margarites village in the Mylopotamos area and when still young was taken in by Arkadi Monastery in order to be given a rudimentary education. His imposing presence with his towering body and long black beard and his shining personality made him stand out early on. Serious, he inspired respect among the monks ensuring cooperation and preventing dissension and strife. At the same he was extremely talkative with a sense of humour, in favour of progress and had a deep knowledge of ecclesiastical music. He chaired the Arkadi Revolutionary Committee and feel heroically during the siege of the Monastery. Although some claim he was killed on the first day of the siege it is almost certain that his death occurred later. According to tradition the flame from his torch was used to set the gunpowder magazine at Arkadi alight.

The historic oak tree was located NE of the Monastery.

about the suppression of their privileges. As a result of this General Assembly held below the historic oak tree at Arkadi a Revolutionary Council was established, based at Arkadi Monastery and chaired by the abbot of the Monastery Hadji Gabriel Marinakis who came from Margarites in the Mylopotamos area. Thus Arkadi became a meeting place attracting other revolutionaries with the result that the attentions of the Turkish authorities were aroused provoking rage in the Commander General of Crete Ishmail Pasha who attempted to dissolve the gathering at Arkadi using every means, threatening that if it was not dissolved the Porte would be forced to dissolve it by violence using the army. At the end of July 1866 a Turkish detachment arrived at Arkadi. Not having managed to arrest the leader of the Revolutionary Council, Abbot Gabriel, the Turks turned to vandalism and destruction of the Church. Since the situation has reached an impasse the Sultan sent Mustafa Pasha to Crete, since he knew the region, in order to ensure a return to peace and order on the island. The enterprise proved fruitless since the revolution was already well under way. Mustafa Pasha too, when he realized that the peaceful route was ineffective, turned to a series of military raids in order to liberate the Turks in various areas of Crete. In order to support the Cretan's military operations a leading solider, Panos Koroneus, was summoned.

The bust of Abbot Gabriel in Margarites (Mylopotamos area).

PANOS KORONEUS

Colonel Panos Koroneus was born in 1809. He grew up on Corfu and studied at Evelpidon Military Academy. He took part in many wars being decorated several times and was twice Greek Minister of Military Affairs. Appointed chief of military operations for Rethymnon by the Cretan General Assembly, he disembarked at Rethymnon in September 1866. Once he reached Arkadi he distributed weapons, encouraged the revolutionaries and began to organize and train a corps of volunteers, while at the same time attempting to increase their number even conscripting some, so that defence of the Monastery would be as effective as possible. In general he considered that the Monastery was not an appropriate site for a revolutionary centre but since he could not persuade others of this, he left Arkadi appointing Ioannis Dimakopoulos in his place.

He arrived in Rethymnon on 24th September 1866 and was proclaimed Commander in Chief of the Rethymnon Division by the Revolutionary Council. Having installed himself at Arkadi, which he made his centre of operations, Panos Koroneus began training military corps consisting of volunteers while at the same time begun reconnaissance into neighbouring and more distant areas in order to measure up the Turkish threat and to meet with and encourage people who could possibly be conscripted into the revolution. His view was that the Monastery was inappropriate in defensive terms both due to ease of access to the plateau and due to the lack of weapons and armaments. His consequent proposals to improve the situation with various infrastructure works were not received well by the majority of the council of chiefs with the result that colonel Panos Koroneus and his men left Arkadi and headed for the Agios Vasilios region. However, before departing he did appoint lieutenant Ioannis Dimakopoulos, from Gortyna in the Peloponnese, as garrison commander and ensured that the process of strengthening the Monastery was set in train with the recruitment and gathering of fighters both at the Monastery itself and in surrounding areas. By 7th November 1866 around 250 men with a remarkable amount of war supplies had gathered at the Monastery. At the end of October 1866 Mustafa Pasha had abandoned

Apokorona fortress in Hania and had begun to march eastwards, initially stopping at Episkopi village, which was completely looted by his men. Without doubt the purpose of this march was the centre of revolutionary activity, Arkadi Monastery, whose destruction in his opinion would almost certainly mean the simultaneous crushing of rebellion on Crete. Following the village of Episkopi, from where a letter was sent to the Revolutionary Committee at Arkadi, that he would arrive within days and that they should be ready to surrender, Mustafa headed for the village of Roustika where he spent the night in the Monastery of the Prophet Elijah (Profitis Ilias) while the army accompanying camped out in the villages of Roustika and Agios Konstantinos. At dawn on 5th November the Turkish army set off for Rethymnon arriving by evening the same day. Shortly thereafter on the night of 7th November - morning of 8th November Mustafa's powerful army, supplemented with all the forces from Rethymnon, Turkish and Egyptian alike, who in total numbered more than 15,000 men, attacked Arkadi Monastery within whose walls were 964 people. Only 325 of them were men. It should be noted that Mustafa himself, although having

A map of Crete dated 1868. Published in Bucharest to be sold to raise funds for the Cretan Struggle. The coloured line shows the route taken by Mustafa Pasha towards Arkadi.

IOANNIS DIMAKOPOULOS

*Lieutenant Ioannis Dimakopoulos was born in
1833 and studied at the Evelpidon Military
Academy. Together with Panos Koroneus he arrived
at Rethymnon in order to assist in organizing the
Cretan Revolution of 1866 from Arkadi, where he
was appointed garrison commander following
Koroneus' departure. He was slaughtered by
the Turks immediately after the holocaust while
being held prisoner.*

accompanied his army at close
quarters on their march through
the area, camped with his staff
in the village of Mesi, a location
with a panoramic view from
where he could monitor the
attack.

Thus, at dawn on 8th November
while mass was being celebrated
in the Monastery's church to
commemorate the feast of the
Archangels, the trumpets of
the Turkish forces were heard
as they approached Arkadi.
The moment they had been
waiting for all those days had
approached. Abbot Gabriel
attempt to rally the crowd
and to   bolster their sense of

patriotism, removing the fear of death since their sacrifice would be for the homeland. Garrison commander Dimakopoulos who was well aware of the meaning of Faith and Homeland did the same. Thus defence of the Monastery began to be organized. The men were dispatched to key points of the Monastery and in response to the question poised by the Turks

Coloured engraving from the Illustrated London News (1867). It shows the Turkish attack on Arkadi Monastery.

whether they would surrender or fight one voice called out that they preferred war. From that moment the pages of the Arkadi Drama began to be written, a story based on the patriotism, heroism and self-denial of the revolutionaries. The Turkish guns began to rain shots in all directions with the main target being the central western gate of the Monastery. Shots were also

focused on the eastern gate. Both were so barricaded from the inside that at the outset it seemed as if it would be difficult to break them down. The first loss was the windmill which the Turks managed to set alight and together with it the fighters who were inside it. But the Turks too suffered heavy losses since many of their men were killed. This was because the revolutionaries were entrenched in the Monastery unlike the Turks who were on open ground and thus easy targets. Despite the fact that things had not gone badly by the end of the first day, and that the besieged hoped they would make it through the night even though the enemy was vastly better armed, it was clear that they had so seek military support from Panos Koroneus who was in the Amari region and from the residents of Mylopotamos. Two fighters from within the Monastery disguised as Turks volunteered to carry the letters requesting assistance. Following this the abbot called on all those besieged whether fighters, the elderly, women and children, to pray in the Monastery's church. Late the same night the 'messengers' returned and with them came the news that access by reinforcements was almost impossible since the Turks had closed almost all roads to the Monastery.

On the second day of the siege, 9th November, things looked bad. Everything pointed to the besieged being in a difficult position with no hope of salvation. Despite knowing this, they kept their morale up and thought only how they might fall in the most heroic manner. Abbot Gabriel urged them once they saw the Turks enter to run to the magazines and set fire to the gunpowder, sacrificing themselves so that the enemy

Lithograph depicting the heroic moment of the holocaust.

Depiction of the Arkadi Drama (Athens, National Art Gallery).

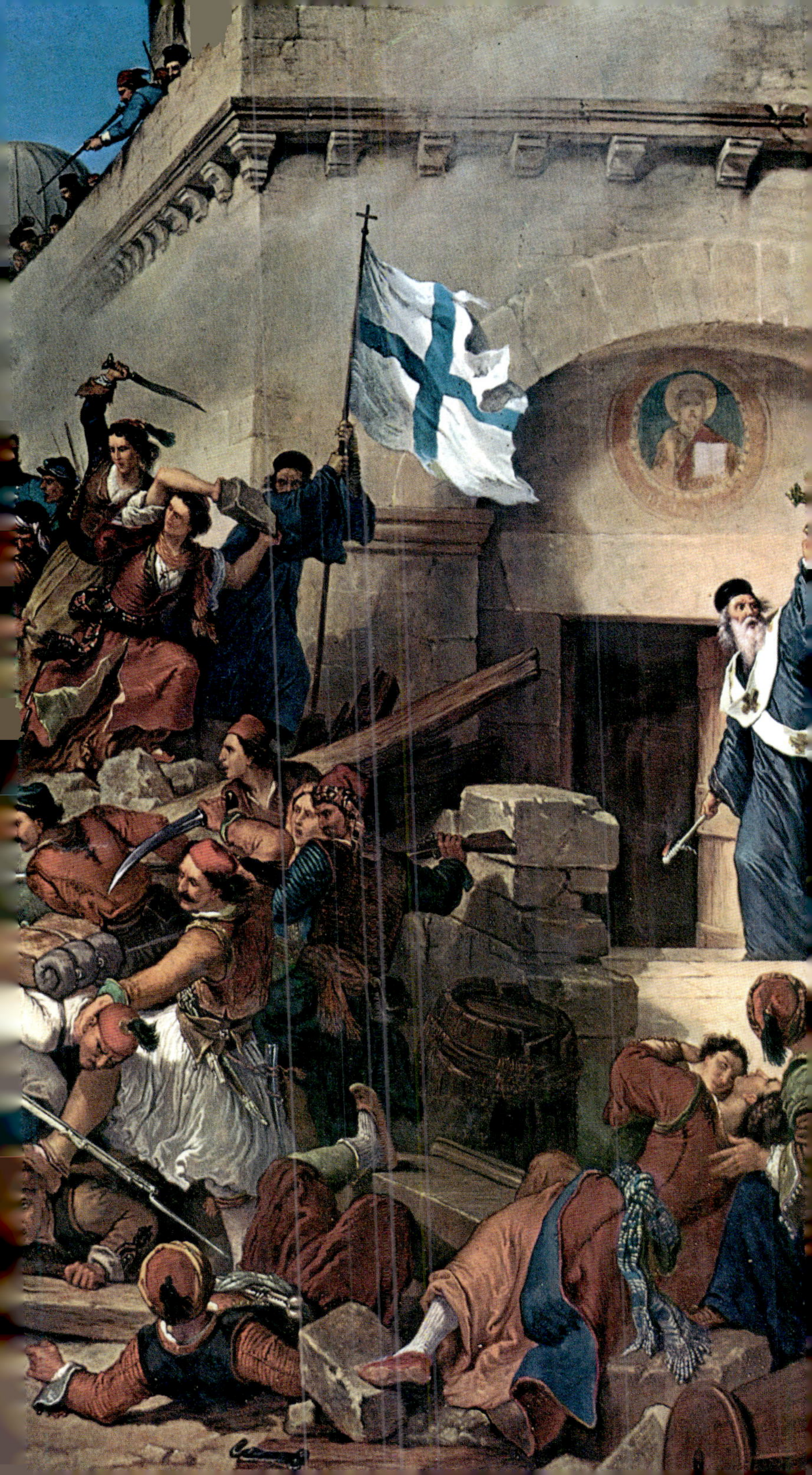

KONSTANTINOS GIAMBOUDAKIS

Kostis Giamboudakis from the village of Adele in Rethymnon province was one of the leading figures in the Arkadi Drama. An imposing figure he stood our for his athletic build, his pride and dignity. According to testimony, during the 1866 revolution he brought his wife and son to his mother's village and left for Arkadi promising that he would fight until the death. And so it was. When the Turks broke down the western gate of the besieged Monastery, Giamboudakis called on all those who wanted to avoid humiliation and brutality to rush to the gunpowder magazines and sacrifice themselves with him. With his very own pistol he ignited the gunpowder causing a massive explosion making heroes of all those who had followed his path of self-sacrifice.

would fall at their hands.

The fighting continued and the Turks for a second consecutive day tried to demolish the Monastery's western gateway. Their efforts were stepped up and they almost achieved their target bringing a large cannon from Rethymnon, the renowned Koustacheila cannon. Having opening a crack in the gate, following successive raids against the Monastery they tried to dishearten the revolutionaries and make them surrender. In vain though because inside the Monastery Abbot Gabriel, garrison commander Dimakopoulos, Kostas Giamboudakis and the heroine Hariklea Daskalaki and other fighters, were urging each other on, racing from place to place encouraging their men not to abandon the battlements. However, the breach in the western gate allowed the enemy to gradually enter the courtyard of the

The statue of Kostis Giamboudakis in Tessaron Martyron Sq. (4 Martyrs Sq.) in Rethymnon.

HARIKLEA DASKALAKI

The heroine Hariklea Daskalaki from the village of Amnatos had three sons, Georgios, Antonios and Konstantinos. All were lost during the Cretan Revolution. She herself was at Arkadi during the siege, urging on the fighters and contributing to the struggle in every possible way. Following the slaughter at Arkadi she was transferred with other prisoners to Rethymnon. Following her liberation she went to Athens to her daughters where she died.

Monastery. The fighting thus moved behind the walls and the struggle was now man on man. When the courtyard had filled with Turks and the battle seemed to be approaching its end, the besieged shut themselves in the gunpowder magazine and the hero Kostas Giamboudakis set it alight causing an explosion and with it the heroic sacrifice of the besieged of Arkadi Monastery. The Turks then proceeded to loot the Monastery burning everything and slaughtering survivors. Even certain men who had remained in the Monastery's refectory unaware of what had happened in the magazines were slaughtered in the most atrocious of ways. The refectory was stained with their blood.

The final scene from the siege: In this depiction the abbot sets light to the gunpowder magazine.

The result of the Turkish attack was tragic. As mentioned above 964 Christians were inside the Monastery including women and children. Of those 114 were taken prisoner, 3-4 escaped and the rest were killed. On the Turkish side no less than 1,500 lost their lives, although there are differences of opinion about the precise number.

Their corpses were either interred at various locations or remain unburied, as was the case with many Christians, and were latter thrown into the nearby gorge. The bones of most Christians were later collected and placed in the windmill which was converted into a resting place for the heroes of the Arkadi Drama. The fate of all those who survived this tragedy was no better than those who had died at Arkadi. According to testimony given by them, immediately after the destruction of Arkadi all 114 of them were imprisoned by the

The bones of the heroes are now kept in the Monastery's ossuary.

Turks and transferred to the city of Rethymnon under terrible conditions. The prisoners were subjected to humiliation not only by the Turkish officers who transported them but also by those who awaited them at the entrance to the city. Stones were thrown and names called. The women, among whom was Hariklea Daskalaki, and

A windmill once stood at the site of the Heroes' Monument.

the children were kept for one week in the Church of the Presentation of the Virgin in the Temple while the men were imprisoned for a whole year under unimaginable conditions of horror and they would never have escaped this were it not for the intervention of the Russian Consul Skouloudis and the Consul General of Russia to Crete who insisted that the Pasha ensure rudimentary hygiene and clothing for the prisoners of Arkadi. Having spent one year in prison the prisoners were released and returned to their villages to continue the Cretan Revolution.

The barbarity of the siege and the unbelievable horror and harshness visited on the prisoners both during their transportation from Arkadi to Rethymnon and during their one year imprisonment are described with spine-tingling precision by the survivors themselves in testimony given afterwards, testimony which not only moves one but is also the most watertight evidence in our effort to piece together the puzzle of the story of the holocaust at Arkadi Monastery. As was only to be expected, the Turks considered the fall of Arkadi to be a great success and celebrated with cannon fire. On the other hand, the indignation which these events caused not only among the Cretans and Greeks but also across all of Europe and even as far as America, was so great

The representative of Russia to Rethymnon, George Skouloudis from Margarites near Mylopotamos.

that we can even speak of major repercussions from the events with a large number of reactions in favour of Greece and Crete. Everywhere where there were Greeks abroad and people of a liberal mindset and an awareness of the rights of man, memorial services were conducted for the repose of the heroes of Arkadi. Funds were raised and a plethora of philhellenic letters

The seal of the Russian Vice Consulate in Rethymnon.

Depiction of the siege of Arkadi and the explosion of the gunpowder magazine (Athens, Gennadius Library).

and articles were written in which Cretan patriotism was praised and the need to liberate Crete stressed. "The Times" of London, the Russian press and leading figures such as Garibaldi and Victor Hugo wrote articles and letters to honour the dead and encourage the Cretans in their struggle. Support was by no means limited solely to declarations. Volunteers arrived on Crete to reinforce the revolution, fighting on the front line themselves while at the same time associations were formed

A poem by E. Vivylakis about Arkadi taken from the Cretan Atlas prepared by the Russian Philhellene Ivan Petrov.

VICTOR HUGO

In his letters in support of the Cretans, Victor Hugo encouraged them to show patience because victory would not be far away. He was optimistic and urged them on, saying that the Cretan Question had been raised and would be resolved. He accurately described the events at Arkadi and stressed that it was no different from the events on Psara or at Mesolongi.

GIUSEPPE GARIBALDI

Although Giuseppe Garibaldi himself never went to Crete quite a few of his supporters urged on by intense philhellenism fought with passion in various battles even giving their own lives. Garibaldi himself in letters stressed the patriotism of the Cretans and wished for liberation.

Busts of the heroes of Arkadi outside the Heroes Monument: Abbot Gabriel, Kostis Giamboudakis, Ioannis Dimakopoulos, Hariklia Daskalaki.

around Europe and America to take care of the women and children of Arkadi.

Three years later in January 1869 a major rebellion broke out which vindicated the many years of Cretan struggles and in particular those who had died at Arkadi. Crete at last was free.

The centuries-old cypress tree in the monastery's courtyard. One can see Turkish gunshot lodged in its trunk.

Immediately after these events the Monastery became a symbol. A ship named Arkadi became legendary because despite the difficulty in docking at Crete's ports, it managed to make 23 sailings to the island in 1867 in order to deliver munitions to the Cretan revolutionaries (Athens, Gennadius Library).

THE MONASTERY'S ARCHITECTURE

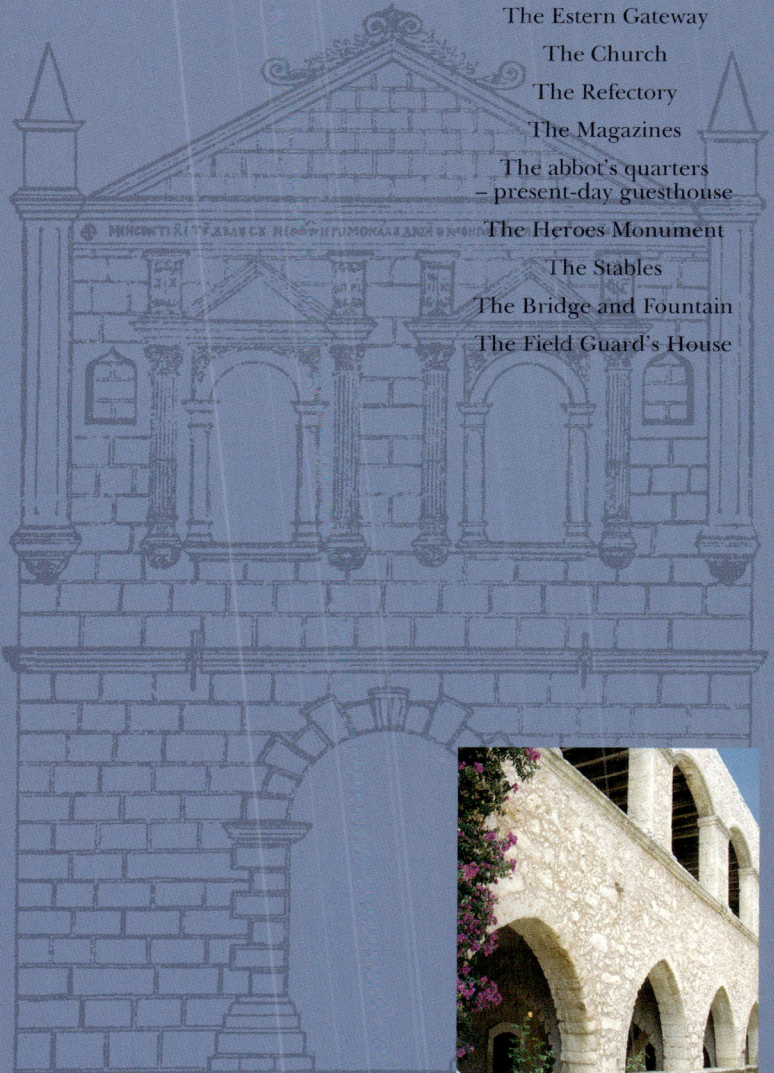

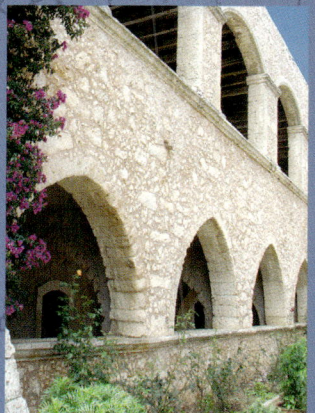

As mentioned in the introduction Arkadi Monastery is built on the plateau with the same name which allowed its architects and builders to create a regular, almost rectangular-shaped courtyard surrounded by walls. These fortress-like walls have sides measuring 78.50 m on the north, 73.50 m on the south, 71.80 m on the east and 67 m on the west. The total area covered by the walled-in area, and within which the Monastery complex was built, is 5,200 m². Inside the walls various buildings have been erected around their sides such as the abbot's quarters, the cells, the kitchen, the refectory, the storerooms, the gunpowder magazine and the guesthouse. A characteristic feature of the curtain walls are the murder holes (for rifles) which are to be found in the upper section of the walls along the southern and eastern sides. Inside the rectangle formed by the curtain walls and the buildings built around their inner sides is the courtyard, in the centre of which is the Monastery's renowned church. The church is not dead centre lying slightly south of the centre.

Access to the Monastery is to be had via two gateways, one to the west and one to the east with smaller doorways, one in the SE corner, two along the northern side and one on the western side.

THE WESTERN GATEWAY AND THE CLOISTERS

The central gateway of the Monastery is that located on its western side and is known as the Rethymnon or Hania gateway since it is oriented towards those areas. The present-day gateway was constructed in 1870 on the site of that which had been built in 1693 and which was destroyed during the Turkish attack and looting of 1866.

According to the inscription which existed at the base of the pediment, as can be seen from the plan dated 1745, the first gateway had been built in 1693 when the abbot of the Monastery was Neophytos Drósas or Drosás. According to a description in a manuscript kept at the Monastery, it was built of stone blocks and in addition to the gateway itself include two windows on the second floor and terminated in a pediment. At the base of the pediment was the inscription:

ΜΝΗΣΘΗΤΙ ΚΥΡΙΕ ΤΟΥ ΔΟΥΛΟΥ ΣΟΥ ΝΕΟΦΥΤΟΥ ΙΕΡΟΜΟΝΑΧΟΥ ΔΡΟΣΑ ΤΟΥ ΚΑΘΗΓΟΥΜΕΝΟΥ ΚΑΙ ΠΑΣΗΣ ΤΗΣ ΕΝ ΧΡΙΣΤΩ ΗΜΩΝ ΑΔΕΛΦΟΤΗΤΟΣ LORD, CARE FOR THE SOUL OF YOUR

SERVANT, MONK NEOPHYTOS DROSAS AND ALL CHRISTIAN BRETHREN

The windows with their triangular lintels were surrounded by fluted columns decorated with lions in relief. On passing the central gate one finds oneself below a vault which leads on into the Monastery's inner courtyard.

To the left and right are arches which lead to the cloisters, in other words the arched, domed stoa along the western side of the curtain walls. This cloister and the one directly above it are a forecourt to the cells both on the lower level and the upper level. The cloisters are 47 m long and 3.40 m wide on both levels. On the lower level the cloister is covered by vaults while on the upper level it has a wooden roof. In both cases there are multiple arched openings looking onto the inner courtyard of the Monastery. The lower level has eight arched openings while the upper level has a series of pillars 2 m high

The monastery bell

Along the eastern part of the monastery's south side, is developed the complex of the so called "Mesokoumia". It's about eight cells in front of which is a corridor roofed with a semicircular vault. As the etymology of the word "mesokoumia" indicates, there was the hospital of the monastery.

with carved, Ionic capitals which are connected by curved arches which form the openings. The areas behind the cloisters on the upper level are the monks' cells while those on the lower level were intended for servants or storage areas.

The upper level on the western side of the monastery with the doorways to the cells, the corridor with its wooden ceiling and the semi-circular openings looking onto the courtyard.

THE EASTERN GATEWAY

On the eastern side of the curtain walls is the Monastery's second gateway which is called the Kastrini Gate since it is oriented towards Heraklion. Heraklion was once also known as Kastro.

The history of the eastern gate is similar to that of the western gate. In this case too the present-day gateway was erected in 1870 on the site of the older one destroyed in 1866 when the Monastery fell to the Turks.

THE CHURCH

In the centre and slightly to the south of the inner courtyard of the Monastery stands the Church, a two-aisled basilica whose

northern aisle is dedicated to the Transfiguration of Christ the Saviour and the southern to Saints Constantine and Helen. According to an inscription which has been preserved at the foot of the bell tower on the church's façade, the

church was built in 1587 and is this part of the works carried out at the time when the Venetians ruled Crete. This fact explains the plethora of renaissance architectural details that immediately confront the visitor looking at the monument.

The façade of the church could be said to be divided into two zones. In the lower zone, which is built of squared off stone blocks in straight rows, the main role is played by four pairs of half-columns resting on high pediments. The decorative solution of double columns is without doubt of gothic origin despite the fact that their individual elements clearly express Roman influences. Above the Corinthian capitals of these half-columns is a Corinthian entablature consisting of architrave, frieze and cornice.

Between the pairs of half columns are three semicircular arches resting on

pilasters. The two end arches have a circle opening within them with floral decoration around their edge and a doorway below while in the central arch there is only a decorative frame. The second zone on the façade is above the Corinthian entablature and includes a series of moldings and oval openings which also have floral decoration around their edges exactly above the circular openings of the lower zone. In the centre of the upper zone of the façade rises the bell tower while at either end are two decorative obelisk inspired by gothic style.

What undoubtedly constitutes the major success of the church is the fact that although it is two-aisled its façade has a uniform composition where a range of architectural elements are harmoniously combined such as gothic arches and obelisks, renaissance floral work, Corinthian molding in late renaissance style and Baroque volutes. The architect of Arkadi surely did not have just taste and skill in providing the proper solutions but had indulged himself in the history of architecture, and in particular in the work of the Renaissance architects Sebastiano Serlio and Andrea Palladio, as one can easily see by comparing the

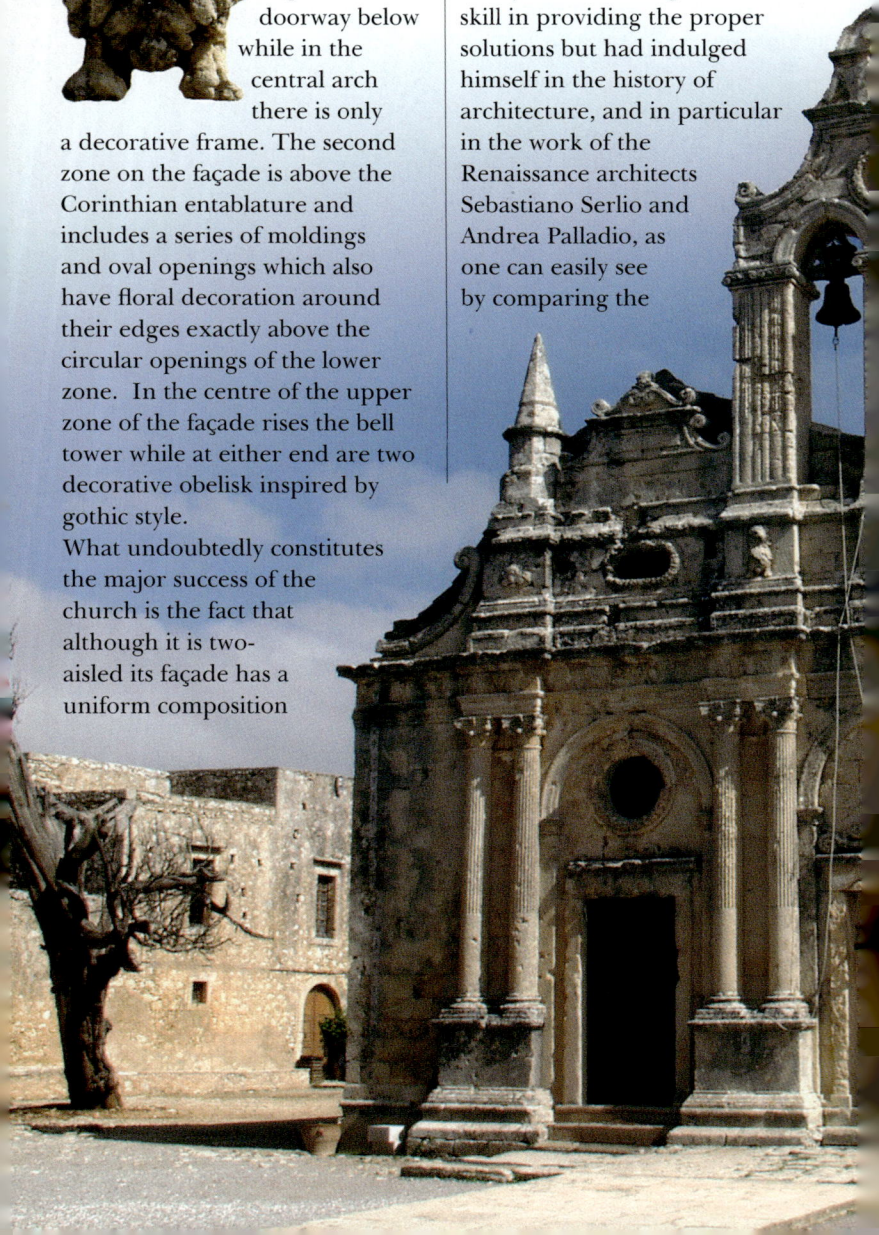

façade of Arkadi with works of the aforementioned leading lights of architecture.

Inside the church, its carved wooden iconostasis was made of cypress wood in 1902. The previous one had been completely destroyed during the Arkadi Drama with the exception of the Cross, the gilded angels and part of the scene depicting Resurrection of Christ which have survived to this day. The plan and icons for the present-day iconostasis where effected by Dionysius, Bishop of Rethymnon and Avlopotamos. Between 1924 and 1927 with the support of the Metropolitan of Crete, Timotheos Veneris, many stabilization projects were carried out around the entire Monastery including work on the interior of the church. In 1933 the floor tiles were replaced while in more recent years the Ephorate of Byzantine Antiquities has carried out research on the interior of the church.

The carved wooden iconostasis in the church built in 1902. The previous one was almost completely destroyed during the holocaust at the monastery.

The monastery's two-aisled church viewed from the east.

THE REFECTORY

Among the buildings on the northern side of the Monastery is the Refectory, in other words the place where monks shared a meal immediately after Mass. The last scene of the Arkadi Drama was played out here since some of those who had remained

The gateway leading from the courtyard towards the refectory. On the keystone in the arch is an inscription dated 1687.

alive following the explosion of the gunpowder magazine were slaughtered here. The traces of bullets and swords which remain to this day on the tables are witness to the barbarity of the fighting.

This building has not undergone any change to its original construction and must have been erected in 1687. Evidence for this

comes from an inscription located above the central doorway which leads to the courtyard outside the refectory. The inscription still bears the name of Abbot Neophytos Drosas:

AXΠZ (1687)
NΦT (Neophytos)
ΔPC   (Drosas)

Upon entering the courtyard on one's left is a small staircase which leads to the roof and a small doorway which once led to the Abbot's quarters. Exactly in front of it, in other words to the north, is the main entrance to the refectory which consists of a doorway with a lintel in the form of a pediment. At the base of the pediment is the inscription:

ΠΑΜΜΕΓΑ ΜΟΧΘΟΝ ΔΕΞΑΙΟ ΒΛΑΣΤΟΥ ΗΓΕΜΟΝΟΙΟ
ΔΕΣΠΟΙΝΑ Ω ΜΑΡΙΑ ΦΙΛΤΡΟΝ ΑΠΕΙΡΕΣΙΟΝ ΑΧΟ

OUR LADY, MARY, ACCEPT THE HARD WORK AND ENDLESS LOVE OF ABBOT VLASTOS 1670

The interior of the refectory is a parallelogram with E-W orientation covering 18.10 m x 4.80 m. It is roofed with a semi-circular vault and has three windows on the northern side and a skylight to the east. The door on the eastern side leads to the kitchen. The tables used to placed lengthwise along the room and on the narrow western side was the Abbot's misericord from where the blessing for the meal was read. On the southern side is a basin decorated with a relief representation of a head.

ΑΥΤΗ Η ΦΛΟΓΑ ΠΑΝΑΨΕ ΜΕΣΑ ΕΔΩ ΣΤΗ ΚΡΥΠΤΗ
ΚΑΙ ΑΠ'ΑΚΡΟΥ Σ'ΑΚΡΟ ΦΩΤΙΣΕ ΤΗ ΔΟΞΑΣΜΕΝΗ ΚΡΗΤΗ
ΗΤΟΝΕ ΦΛΟΓΑ ΤΟΥ ΘΕΟΥ ΜΕΣΑ ΕΙΣ ΤΗΝ ΟΠΟΙΑΝ
ΚΡΗΤΕΣ ΟΛΟΚΑΥΤΩΘΗΣΑΝ ΓΙΑ ΤΗΝ ΕΛΕΥΘΕΡΙΑΝ
ΕΤΕΙ ΣΩΤΗΡΙΩ
✝ Ο ΡΕΘΥΜΝΗΣ ΚΑΙ ΑΥΛΟΠΟΤΑΜΟΥ ΤΙΜΟΘΕΟΣ Μ.ΒΕΝΕΡΗΣ

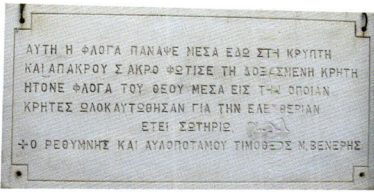

THE GUNPOWDER MAGAZINE

The magazine is located in the NE corner of the Monastery and was intended to hold munitions. However, under Turkish rule the monk's transferred these to the wine store in the northeast corner of the courtyard since being located on the lower level it ensured more protection. The gunpowder magazine

is an elongated vaulted structure 21 m long and 5.40 m wide and following the explosion on 9th November 1866 the entire building was destroyed apart from a small section of the west wall. The following inscription was placed on the eastern wall in 1930:

THIS FLAME LIT
INSIDE THIS CRYPT
WHICH SHONE ON GLORIED
CRETE FROM END TO END
WAS THE FLAME OF GOD
BY WHICH THE CRETANS
ENDURED A HOLOCAUST
TO BE FREE

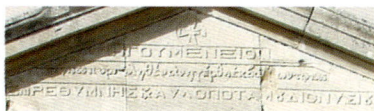

THE ABBOT'S QUARTERS (PRESENT-DAY GUESTHOUSE)

The building constituting the present-day guesthouse on the northern side of the Monastery was once the Abbot's Quarters. These quarters were completely destroyed when set alight in 1866. The old building consisted of two floors. On the ground floor was the kitchen, refectory and a small room which served as a holding cell. A staircase inside the refectory led to the upper floor where the main hall, known as the Meeting Room, was located. Monks met here after mass. There were another four rooms on this floor: the deacon's room, a servant's room, the sacrarium and a room dedicated to the Virgin Miliotissa.

Following its catastrophe in 1866 the Abbot's Quarters were almost completely destroyed and remained in ruins for a long period of time due to the financial problems faced by the Monastery. In 1894 Abbot Gabriel Manaris, having requested permission from the Metropolis of Moscow, raised funds in many cities throughout Russia over a period of two years. He gathered enough money, ecclesiastical vessels and vestments for the Monastery. However, demolition of the old Abbot's Quarters and erection of the present-day guesthouse on the same site commenced much later in 1904 under Dionysios, Bishop of Rethymnon and Avlopotamos. This is attested by the inscription on the pediment above the main entrance. The new, two-storey building which was completed within two years is laid out as follows: a central entrance crowned by a pediment leads into an inner paved courtyard with a stone internal staircase leading to the second floor where the reception room, the Bishop of Rethymnon's chamber and the guests' quarters are located. On the ground floor is the kitchen, refectory, food storerooms and other rooms for accommodating guests.

THE HEROES' MONUMENT

Outside the Monastery to the west is the Heroes' Monument. This is an octagonal building in which the bones of those who fell during the siege of 1866 have been placed. This building was initially a windmill and was later used as a storehouse. It was converted to an ossuary after 1866 and took on its final form around 1910 under the guidance of Dionysios, Bishop of Rethymnon.

THE STABLES

Another building located outside the Monastery to the west again is the Stable block. This block was built in 1714 under Abbot Neophtyos Drosas. As the inscription at the entrance attests it was used as a barn and stables for beasts of burden and also had rooms for the animal handlers to live in.

The stable block has an overall façade length of 17.20 m, is 23.90 m deep and its walls are 1 m thick. It has three vaulted chambers with a façade length of 4.40 m each.

THE BRIDGE AND FOUNTAIN

Shortly before arriving at the Monastery one comes upon a bridge built of shaped stone blocks in the form of an arch spanning a small gorge. According to the inscription built into the bridge it was erected in 1685. The text of the inscription is set out below in Greek with an English translation provided:

ΜΝΗΣΘΗΤΙ ΚΥΡΙΕ ΤΟΥ ΔΟΥΛΟΥ
ΣΟΥ ΝΕΟΦΥΤΟΥ ΙΕΡΟΜΟΝΑΧΟΥ
ΔΡΟΣΑ ΤΟΥ ΚΑΘΗΓΟΥΜΕΝΟΥ
ΚΑΙ ΠΑΣΗΣ ΤΗΣ ΕΝ ΧΡΙΣΤΩ
ΗΜΩΝ ΑΔΕΛΦΟΤΗΤΟΣ

LORD, CARE FOR THE SOUL OF YOUR SERVANT, MONK NEOPHYTOS DROSAS AND ALL CHRISTIAN BRETHREN, MARCH 1693

Near the bridge is a fountain built in 1918 by Abbot Ambrosius Zacharakis in order to carry water there from the older fountain and cistern in the location known as Kamara which had been built in 1651 by Abbot Gerasimos Vlastos. The older fountain bears the inscription:

The stone bridge with its inscription.

ΑΦΘΟΝΑ ΤΗΣΔΕ ΝΑΜΑΤΑ
ΚΡΗΝΗΣ ΔΩΚΕΝ ΟΔΙΤΑΙΣ
ΑΧ – ΒΛΑΣΤΟΥ ΗΓΟΥΜΕΝΟΥ
ΕΒΡΕΣΙΣΙ ΟΞΥΤΑΤΗ – ΝΑ΄

MAY THIS FOUNTAIN, AN IMPORTANT DISCOVERY OF ABBOT VLASTOS, PROVIDE BOUNTIFUL WATER TO TRAVELLERS. 1651

The water fountain with its inscription.

THE FIELD GUARD'S HOUSE

Generally speaking these huts are places where Field Guards reside, in other words the people who guard the vineyards. In this case this term is used to mean the group of cells located in the southeast of the Monastery and which before 1866 were used to produce wine and as accommodation for the Monastery's shepherds.

THE MUSEUM

THE MUSEUM

The Monastery's museum is located in the western wing. It contains a range of objects and relics of priceless historical value. In addition to the banner of the Revolution its treasures include ecclesiastical vessels and hieratical vestments, handwritten codices, post-Byzantine icons, weapons and a series of personal items belonging to the Monastery's heroic abbot, Gabriel Marinakis. The aforementioned relics were rescued from the destruction which took place in 1866 thanks to the monks who had hidden them before the siege in the walls of their cells. Immediately after the siege they were handed over to Archimandrite Dorotheos Stavridis who hid them in some cave in the village of Platania near Amari and thereafter they were returned to

The Virgin Glykophiloussa. A portable icon from the first half of the 18th century. The inscription on the left reads Succor of the Despondent.

Vestments belonging to abbot Gabriel, the stole is richly illustrated and set in the embroidery is an inscription dated 1724.

Glasses bearing Abbot Gabriel's monogram.

the Monastery, where they are now exhibited in its museum. The vestments which date to the 17th and 18th centuries are all made of valuable textiles and decorated with theological scenes, embroidered with gold, silver and coloured silk threads. The choice of scenes, the perfection and balance of the compositions, the harmony and wealth of the colours used and the fine work involved are all evidence that a leading gold embroidery workshop must have been in operation at the Monastery producing vestments from the 17th until the 19th century in which the monks themselves must have worked. Signatures together with the phrase "done by my hand…" added to the embroidery attest this. One such example is a pair of kneeling figures together with Christ and the 12 Apostles and the inscription "By done my hand Parthenius, Monk and Abbot of Arkadi from Kiotza, 1861". According to Byzantine expert, Professor N.B. Drandakis, who has published a work on the ecclesiastical embroidery from Arkadi Monastery, the style of this embroidery is sometimes fully in line with Byzantine tradition and in other cases with western tradition while the images presented as a rule follow Byzantine tradition with some loans from Turkish art.

As mentioned above, in addition to the vestments, another valuable group of items on display at Arkadi Monastery's museum is the manuscripts. As can be seen from notes and signatures in manuscripts which have survived to date in various libraries, during the 16th century Arkadi was an important manuscript copying centre. Most of the manuscripts were

The Royal Doors from old iconostasis depicting the Apostles Peter and Paul and a scene from the gospel in the upper section (16th century).

St. George the Trophy-bearer, 17ᵗʰ c.

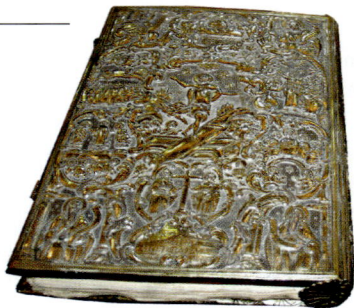

A holy gospel.

play a role as a cultural centre disseminating knowledge in an age when typography had not yet become widespread. The Monastery's museum also contains a wealth of holy vessels, crosses in various sizes made of a range of precious and semi-precious metals, silver and gilded Gospels, chalices, gold reliquaries of saints and silver

unfortunately destroyed when the Monastery fell in 1866. This role of the Monastery as a coping centre is attested by a letter from monk Symeon Halkiopoulos from Arkadi Monastery to the abbot of Chrysopigi Monastery, Neophytos Skordilos. In this letter Symeon Halkiopoulos asks for forgiveness for the delay in copying and embellishing the Antioch Pandectus Codex which included advice to abbots on how monks should be taught. Without doubt this was just one of the many copying activities of the Monastery and in this way it was able to

The Resurrection of Christ. One of the few sections of the old iconostasis which have survived.

incense holders.

Nonetheless one of the most important exhibits in the museum with outstanding historical value is the Banner which was raised above the besieged Monastery on 8th November over the central gateway. It is made of white linen and contains a depiction of the Transfiguration of Christ the Saviour.

Its state of preservation with numerous bullet holes from enemy fire is clear evidence of the brutality of that day. The fact that this historical banner of the Monastery is today to be found among the museum's exhibits is matter of pure chance since immediately after the siege it followed what was a quite adventurous fate. After the end of looting it was seized by a Turkish officer who took it with him and hid it in Heraklion. Some years later in 1870 when it was considered well and truly lost the Turk handed it over to monk Symeon Gavras who in turn, overcome with emotion, returned it to its rightful place, Arkadi Monastery, where it remains the eternal symbol of patriotism, heroism and self-sacrifice.

The banner from the Arkadi rebellion.

The Refectory door with bullet marks. The last scene of the Arkadi Drama was played out here. All those who had remained alive from the gunpowder magazine explosion were slaughtered here.

THE TRAVELLERS

THE TRAVELLERS

A large number of foreign travellers visited Greece from the 14th century onwards. Their numbers increased during the 18th and 19th centuries.

Their primary aim was to collect information about the culture of the area, the natural environment, customs and lifestyles. Crete, with its wealth of archaeological finds and history, attracted quite a few of them and, of course, Arkadi Monastery was a favourite stopping points on their travels.

It is cited in their writing with details of its architecture, finances, monastic life, agricultural produce depending on the interests and education of each traveller.

Let us now look at what certain of the most important travellers who visited Arkadi had to say about it.

JOSEPH PITTON DE TOURNEFORT in his work **A Voyage into the Levant,** vol. 1, p. 39-40, London 1718, wrote:

"On 30th June we reached Arkadi twelve miles from Rethymnon to sleep. It seems that this Monastery, which is the most beautiful and richest on the island, retains its

The city of Rethymnon viewed from the east. J. Pitton de Tournefort.

A
VOYAGE
INTO THE
LEVANT:
Perform'd by Command of the Late *French* King.

CONTAINING

The Antient and Modern STATE of the Iſlands of the *Archipelago* ; as alſo of *Conſtantinople*, the Coaſts of the *Black Sea*, *Armenia*, *Georgia*, the Frontiers of *Perſia*, and *Aſia Minor*.

WITH

PLANS of the principal Towns and Places of Note ; an Account of the Genius, Manners, Trade, and Religion of the reſpective People inhabiting thoſe Parts : And an Explanation of Variety of Medals and Antique Monuments.

Illuſtrated with Full Deſcriptions and Curious Copper-Plates of great Numbers of Uncommon Plants, Animals, *&c.* And ſeveral Obſervations in Natural Hiſtory.

By M. TOURNEFORT, of the Royal Academy of Sciences, Chief Botaniſt to the late *French* King, *&c.*

To which is Prefix'd,

The Author's LIFE, in a Letter to M. Begon : As alſo his Elogium, pronounc'd by M. Fontenelle, before a publick Aſſembly of the Academy of Sciences.

Adorn'd with an Accurate MAP of the Author's Travels, not in the *French* Edition : Done by Mr. Senex.

In TWO VOLUMES.

LONDON,

Printed for D. BROWNE, A. BELL, J. DARBY, A. BETTESWORTH, J. PEMBERTON, C. RIVINGTON, J. HOOKE, R. CRUTTENDEN and T. COX, J. BATTLEY, E. SYMON. M. DCC. XVIII.

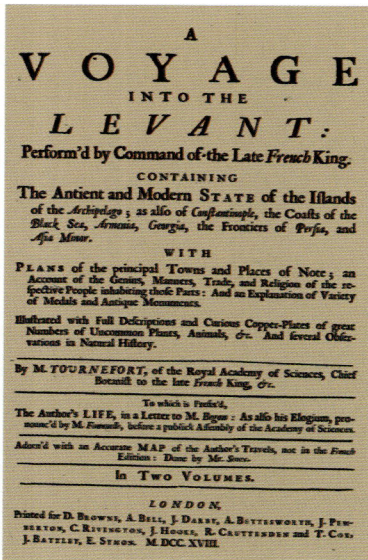

name from the ancient city of Arkadia mentioned by Seneca, Pliny and Stephen the Geographer. It is nonetheless paradoxical that both Seneca and Pliny rely on Theophrastus to make mention of an unbelievable fact, that following destruction of this ancient city, all its wells dried up, only to bubble forth again when the city was rebuilt. Once Christianity had come to prevail, Arkadia was honoured being recognized as the See of the third metropolitan on the island. All that remains of that age is a large Monastery, built on a plateau, like an embankment atop a hill, among the foothills of Mt. Ida. In order for one to reach this place one must pass through a charming valley with water melon fields, vines and cultivated land covered, where it remains uncultivated, by many species of trees and shrubs. Water flows into this valley from all directions and everywhere one can find traces of the ancient city described by Strabo.

The building at Arkadi is large and well constructed. The Katholikon (central church) has two aisles, decorated with gothic wall paintings. Amazing if one thinks that the ancient Greeks managed to imitate nature so faithfully in their art only to end up themselves imitated by the Goths, despite the latter's lack of skill! Perhaps because the beautiful requires so much care. Almost 100 monks live in the Monastery while another 200 farmers live in its dependencies. The Monastery's abbot, an intellectual and well-built man, received us with hospitality. Since those who hold such ranks are usually serious and respectable people, guests do not dare to offer them money in recompense for their hospitality. They limit themselves to leaving only a few coins on the tray with the holy communion that the monks produce following the end of mass.

The Monastery's cellars are some of its most interesting parts. The wine cellar contains more than 200 barrels. The best wine has the abbot's name marked on the barrel and no monk would dare to touch it without permission. In order to bless the cellar, every year after harvesting the grapes the abbot recites a prayer in line with the Orthodox dogma chanting *Lord God show mercy on your servant, cast your eye on this wine and those who drink it. Bless our barrels as you blessed Jacob's well, Siloam's font and the wine of your Holy Apostles. Lord, you who chose to attend the wedding feast at Cana, where in changing the water into wine you revealed all your glory to the eyes of the faithful, send your Holy Spirit and bless this wine in your Holy Name, Amen.*

The Monastery's dependencies stretch north as far as the coast and south to the peak of Mt. Ida. We were assured that this year the monks had produced 400 measures (equivalent to around 7.68 metric tons) of oil even though they left half the crop unharvested due to lack of hands at olive picking. Below Arkadi towards the coast lies Arseni Monastery. We were told it was a most beautiful Monastery. We had no time though to visit it."

• • •

RICHARD POCOCKE in his book **A Description of the East and Some other Countries**, vol. II, part I, 259, London 1745, wrote:

"Four miles on (from Ancient Eleftherna) we passed by the ruined Monastery of St.

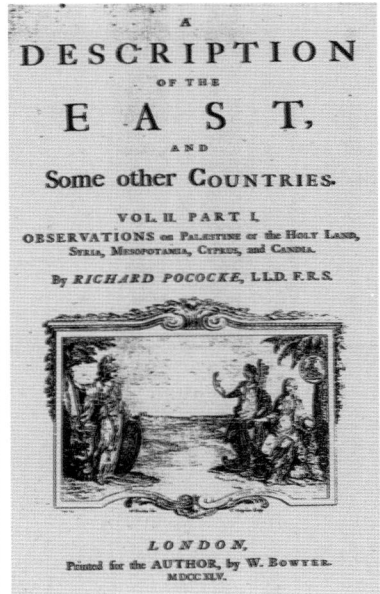

A

DESCRIPTION

OF THE

E A S T,

AND

Some other COUNTRIES.

VOL. II. PART I.

OBSERVATIONS on PALESTINE or the HOLY LAND, SYRIA, MESOPOTAMIA, CYPRUS, and CANDIA.

By *RICHARD POCOCKE*, LL.D. F.R.S.

LONDON,
Printed for the AUTHOR, by W. BOWYER.
MDCCXLV.

Anthony which belongs of Arkadi Monastery. Immediately thereafter we reached a small plain between some hills whose perimeter is approximately 4 miles and in whose centre lies the great Monastery of Arkadi built during the time of Venetian rule. It is a charming structure built around an extensive courtyard. They have a very fine refectory and in the centre of the courtyard a very pretty church with a wonderful façade in the Venetian architectural style. The Monastery has a large income, more than one hundred monks and around twenty priests. The abbot of the Monastery welcomed me with great politeness and led us to accommodation intended for strangers. The abbot always came and dined with me."

F. W. Sieber, in his book
**Travels in the Island of Crete
in the year 1817**, p. 53-55,
London 1823, described Arkadi
as follows:

*"…we could make out the
grandiose Monastery surrounded
by pines and cypress trees.
The clatter of horse's hooves
on the stone flags aroused the
monks at the Monastery who were
greatly surprised at the sight of
a European who had 15 years to
appear since they had expected
only the Abbot. There were no
Turks at the Monastery. After the
looting they had left and thus my
welcome was more pleasant…Mt.
Ida was not fully visible the
next day and a cloud of fog
surrounded the entire Monastery
(since Arkadi lies 202 feet
above sea level). The walls were
moist and I seemed that I have
come during the wettest season.
Although it was flowering time
almost no flowers had bloomed
at Arkadi. The ancient city of
Arkadia was undoubtedly at the
high point were the Monastery
lies. In all likelihood it was not
very large since only with great
difficulty could a mountainous
area support an extensive
population. Among the so-
called ancient cities one might
suppose that only Gortyna,
Knossos, Kydon, Ieraptyna, Lytos,
Praesos, Aptera, Rithymna,
and a few others, could truly be
characterized as cities. If Crete*
*was nonetheless known as the isle
of one hundred cities this must
have included smaller settlements
which were characterized as
cities only because Crete always
included fiefs surrounded by
walls…
The monasteries of Crete are
excellently laid out. There is
no doubt that the ruins of the
ancient city of Arkadia were
used in building this charming
Monastery. It was built by the
Venetian conquerors almost 235
years ago. The church is dark
and stands in the centre of a
paved courtyard surrounded by
cypress trees. Most of the cells
have been converted into barns.
The refectory intended for a
large number of people, with its
beautiful tables, remains empty.
Tournefort mentions that there
were around 100 priests at the
Monastery and almost 200 monks
who busied themselves in the
fields and vineyards. Today there
are no more than 8 priests and
12 monks. They have a lovely,
spacious cellar and the best wine
on the whole island known as
Malvazia taken from the name
of the village Malevizi next to
Candia. When the Venetians
ruled the island large quantities
of this wine were produced
in Rethymnon and Candia.
Production was done by boiling
the grapes in copper cauldrons as
I saw for myself at the Monastery.
Today, though it is extremely rare
and is produced only at Arkadi*

where the vineyards are at high altitudes and produce wonderful grapes. Today such wine is not produced much at all, not even at Malevizi …. A large quantity of wine and corn is produced since the soil is farmed in a good way and work carried out on the fields as normal. The harvest is rich and yet the Monastery has debts. Its estates extend as far as the foothills of Mt. Ida and the valley of Rethymnon, near the sea. The abbot of the Monastery is forced to go regularly to Rethymnon to settle debts and financial obligations.

The abbot drew my attention to the ruins of the library which the Monastery kept in an old room without windows. He spoke such words to me about it that I wished to visit it immediately. The sorrowful remains of that library were in large part classical writers in a sorry state. There were approximately 1000 volumes. I had never seen books in such a state. Most were almost useless. Together with theological works were books by Pindar, Petrarch, Virgil, Dante, Homer, Strabo, Thucydides, Diodorus, all muddled together. One could not make out Aristophanes and Euripides and the best editions of those and other classics were in a terrible condition…"

Arkadi Monastery as seen by Edward Lear. 1876

ROBERT PASHLEY in his work **Travels in Crete** (London 1837, p. 187 & p. 239) mentions Arkadi Monastery twice. One reference is to the relationship with the ancient city of Arkadia where he comments on the remarks and hypotheses of other travellers, while the other relates to his visit to the Monastery.

In relation to the first matter he wrote,

"Tournefort, who pays less attention than Dr. Cramer to the purely topographical indications of the ancient writers, upon reaching the most beautiful and richest Monastery on the island, at least fifty miles west of Knossos,

decided that it was the remains of the ancient city which, as he says, has retained its name. Moreover, Sieber also claims that without doubt the Monastery is located at the site of the ancient city. This hypothesis is so irrational that it does not even merit rebuttal. Only the extensive learning of the author of "Description of Ancient Greece", whose view is equally unfounded and as without basis as that of Tournefort and Sieber, incites me to delay my reader with an examination of its location…" The description of the Monastery from Pashley's visit is limited to the following brief comments, "Following half an hour's climb (from Petra Nero spring) we

The inner courtyard of the monastery with its Katholikon, Pashley, Travels in Crete, 1837.

could see Arkadi Monastery in a small plain surrounded by many pine trees. On the lintel is an inscription, contemporary with the founding of the Monastery I suppose which mentions monk Neophytos, abbot of the Monastery."

• • •

The geologist VITTORIO SIMONELLI is yet another traveller who visited Crete and wrote a work entitled **Candia, Ricordi di Escursione** published in 1897. In relation to Arkadi Monastery he reported,

"Arkadi Monastery was once renowned for the extent and fertility of its estates. Arkadi's wine cellar, Tournefort tells us, is the most beautiful and well-preserved part of the entire Monastery. It contains at least two hundred barrels of wine while those with the best wine are marked with the abbot's name, who blesses it each year with a special prayer for this purpose. The reason for the present-day reputation of Arkadi Monastery is very different. It is the glorious Monastery mentioned by Victor Hugo in his famed letter replying to Zymvrakakis: the heroic Monastery which

resisted like a fortress and fell like a volcano. Rather than surrender to the Turks the revolutionaries who had sought refuge there in '66 preferred to blow themselves up. The abbot himself, the renowned abbot Gabriel, ignited the gunpowder magazine himself. Today the monks, instead of showing the wine cellar, show visitors the marks left by Turkish artillery fire, still fresh on the façade of the church and the trees in the courtyard. They shows the ruins under which those under attack and defending themselves were buried as well as the flag – now completely in tatters – which fluttered on that memorable day."

The façade of the Katholikon. Drawing by Vittorio Simonelli.

BIBLIOGRAPHY

DRANDAKIS N. B., Εκκλησιαστικά κεντήματα της Μονής Αρκαδίου, *Πεπραγμένα Β΄ Διεθνούς Κρητολογικού Συνεδρίου*, τομ. Α', Αθήναι 1967, σ. 297-343

HADJIDAKIS JOSEPH, *Περιήγησις εις Κρήτην*, εν Ερμουπόλει 1881

MANOUSAKAS, M., Άγνωστα Κεφάλαια της παλαιότερης ιστορίας του Αρκαδίου, *Νέα Εστία*, τ. 949/1966

MARANGOUDAKIS, D., Bishop of Pe=a, *Το Ιερόν και Ηρωικόν της Κρήτης Αρκάδι*, 1966

PASHLEY ROBERT, *Travels in Crete*, London 1837

POCOCKE RICHARD, *A Description of the East and Some other Countries*, London 1745

PREVEALAKIS, PANDELIS, *Παντέρμη Κρήτη*, Αθήνα 1945

PREVEALAKIS, PANDELIS, *Το Ηφαίστειο*, Αθήνα 1962

PROVATAKIS, THEOHARIS, *Το Αρκάδι, Ιστορία, Τέχνη, Παράδοση*

PSILAKIS, NIKOS, *Τα Μοναστήρια της Κρήτης*, 1986

SIEBER FRANZ WILHELM, *Travels in the Island of Crete in the year 1817*, London 1823

SIMONELLI VITTORIO, *Candia - Ricordi di escursione*, Parma 1897

TOURNEFORT JOSEPH PITTON DE, *Relction d' un voyage du Levant*, Paris 1717

VENERIS, TIMOTHEOS, *Το Αρκάδι διά των Αιώνων*, 1940